The Publisher's Microsoft Word

Robert Stetson

ISBN-10:   1481251481

ISBN-13: 978-1481251488

By   Robert J Stetson
Copyright © 2010 Robert Stetson
All Rights Reserved

TABLE OF CONTENTS

Preface

The 7 magic areas

For those of us who write books, Microsoft Word 2010 has 7 magic areas we use to get the format just right.

I'm going to take you through each of the areas and show you exactly how to format your document so that your final book will pass the formatting requirements of the publisher. If you use this guide effectively the final book can look like the books made by the big 6 printing houses.

Things such as the "gutter" and facing pages along with headers, footers and the opening section numbered "i" through "iv" and so forth, followed by the main section being numbered "1" through "212" etc.

Getting the Table of Contents right is one of the primary problems writers have when releasing their books. Many writers make a good table of contents only to edit the book or change the margins and forget to recreate the table of contents. ALWAYS, redo the table of contents LAST before releasing the document.

Let's begin the journey through the Microsoft Word software and see how it's done, and why.

Home

This section is called "Home" because it's the foundation area for creating a document.

One of the biggest problems people have with upgrading their MS Word programs isn't learning the new features and functions, it's finding out where they put all of the old stuff. Microsoft has a habit of relocating the functionality in their programs when they rewrite them.

Once you get used to the new layout, you will discover that it's easy to use. The new functionality adds greatly to the quality of your finished product.

In this step by step tutorial, I have included as many screen shots as needed to help you locate the knobs and buttons in the word program.

Once you know where everything is and what it does, the rest is intuitive.

Font

The first area we'll talk about is the "Font" area. This is basic to any and all writing. In the upper left of the area you find the two boxes with the drop down menus for selecting the font style and font size.

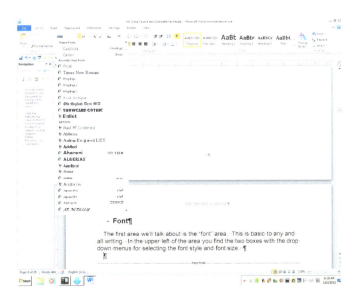

The Font drop down menu is shown above.

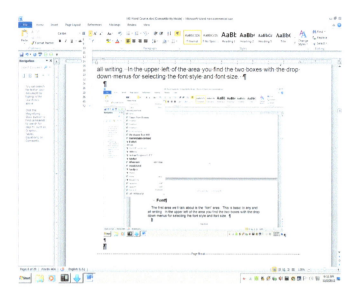

The Font Size drop down menu is shown above.

Notice that in the lower right hand corner of the Font area there is a small square with an arrow pointing down and to the right. Every area on every page will have this square and it opens a popup box allowing characteristic changes in the attributes of this area. The screen below is an example of the popup box that results when this "Expansion Icon" is clicked on.

Note that every time I refer to the "Expansion Icon", I am referring to this Icon in the lower right of the area we are working in.

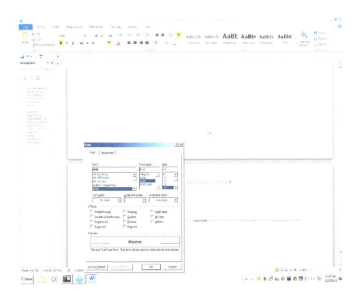

In the screen shot above, we are looking at the popup resulting from clicking on the Expansion Icon in the Font area.

The popup isn't just a repeat of the Icons in the area. The popup offers a great deal more options for controlling the characteristics of the font, as you can see by the check boxes. The window in the popup box shows the current state of the font and underneath the window is a description of the type of font represented.

If things get really strange and you're not sure how to fix it, there is the option in the bottom of the popup marked, "Set As Default" that will return everything back to where you started.

Paragraph

The Paragraph area allows you to control the attributes of the paragraph you're working on. If you want to apply the same attributes to the entire document, then highlight the entire document before selecting the attribute, such as left and right margin justification for example.

There are some interesting options listed here. Let's look at a couple that you will be using from time to time.

If you select a list of items, for instance the list shown below,

Rat
Cat
Mat

You can create a bulleted list by highlighting the list and clicking on the bullet Icon in the upper left of the Paragraph area, like so,

- Rat
- Cat
- Mat

You can number them as well by using the numbered Icon next to it.

Up near the upper right there is an Icon with an "A" and a "Z" with a down arrow. This will create an alpha-numeric sorting of the list. A popup menu will appear as shown below.

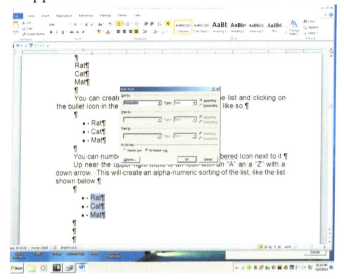

The popup enables you to control the way the list is sorted. I have selected "Ascending and the list is sorted as shown below,

- Cat
- Mat
- Rat

In the lower left of the Paragraph area, there is an assortment of horizontal lines meant to represent the placement of text on the page. The screenshot showing the Paragraph area is shown below. The one with the right and left edges (last one on the right) is for justified right and left margins. Take any book from any shelf anywhere and the left and right margins are justified. A ragged right margin looks terrible!

The Expansion Icon in the Paragraph area (on the lower right hand side) opens a popup box that performs special formatting attributes that you're going to need every time you publish a book.

This is one of the more important places when publishing a document, especially on Smashwords where formatting issues are much stricter than on Amazon.

With Amazon, as long as the document meets some rather broad formatting requirements, the ultimate appearance of the document is left to the writer.

On Smashwords, the formatting is scrupulously examined and changes are required in order to meet the standards for their broader distribution.

The popup is shown in the screenshot below.

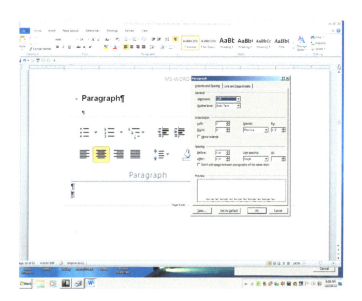

Because this popup is so important, let's blow it up and take a closer look at the options. It will make your overall document look much more professional than just using the MS Word defaults.

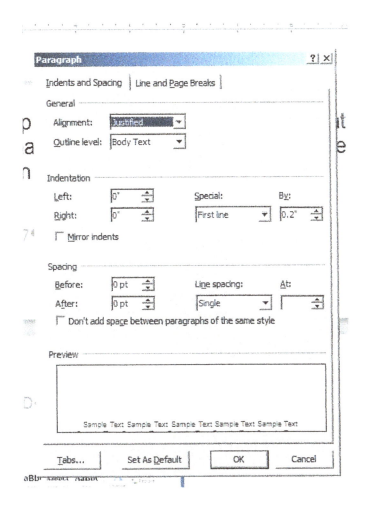

The part of the popup labeled "Indentation" is used to control the start of each paragraph. Under "Special" I select the "First Line" to set the depth of the indentation for each paragraph. You're going to want to select the best paragraph indentation for most books, which I find, at least for me, to be a "0.02" indent (The one used here in this book).

When using a paragraph indentation, there should never be a space between the paragraphs. It's not needed and makes the book look amateurish.

I do, however, use spaces between text and illustrations; otherwise I find the illustration looks crowded. Also, I use spaces to set text apart from the other items needing to be isolated.

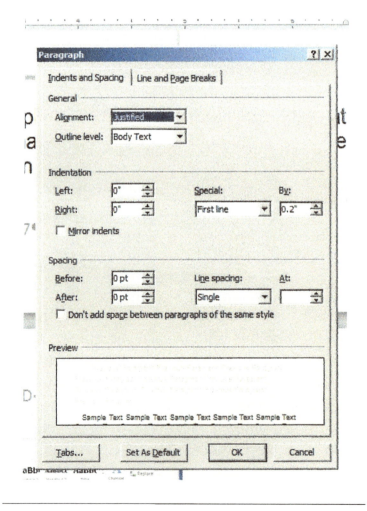

Under the section labeled, "Spacing" you will sometimes need to insert a space between paragraphs.

Textbooks are sometimes better reading with no indentation and a space between paragraphs. How-to books are also sometimes done with this format.

Never combine spacing between paragraphs with paragraph indentation. Here again, it makes the book look amateurish.

Styles

The "Style" area is one you will almost always use, unless you're not creating a document with a table of contents, or unless you're creating a menu for Smashwords.

The actual Table of Contents is generated in the special area called "References" which we will get to later on, but the References area looks to the Styles area for information to create the actual Table of Contents menu.

You can have as many levels of categories and subcategories as needed in a Table of Content. If you look at the Table of Contents in this book, you will see two levels of Content. The first level is "Heading 1" and the indented Content is "Heading 2" information.

All of the standard text in a chapter should be of the style called "Normal. If you look at the Styles area, the box called "Normal" would have a yellow square around it to show that this is the style for the selected text. When you select your Chapter headings, You should make your "Chapter" headings a "Header 1" format. Once you get the chapter heading for the first chapter set up, you can put the mouse pointer on the "Header 1" box and right click.

The top item on the drop down list is "Update Heading 1 to Match Selection". By doing this, from now on every time you click on Heading 1, the text layout and formatting will be the same as the one you selected for the first chapter. It saves you from having to tweak every chapter heading in the book to match.

THE PUBLISHER'S MICROSOFT WORD

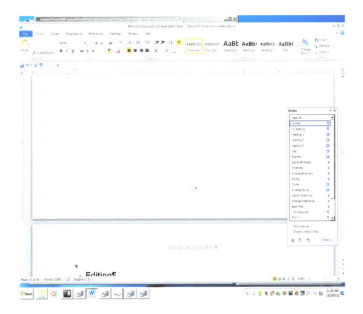

Since there is limited room on the Styles area, clicking on the Expansion Icon will produce the popup shown in the screenshot above. This popup lists every available type of Style available and can be used to select the style for the text you have highlighted. For ordinary publications you will probably never need this feature.

Editing

This is one of the most important areas in MS Word. Use it often and it will save you hours of scanning through the document looking for things you need to add, delete or change.

It doesn't jump out at you, but if you look to the far right of the top banner, you can see the little Icon area labeled "Editing".

In MS Word 2010, they did something special. There is a section that appears down the left hand side of the document, and it enables you to do a number of different search techniques.

Find Function

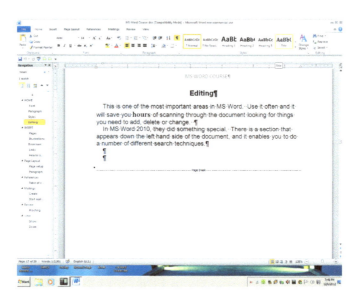

In the Icon area called Editing the word "Find" will open the "Navigation" box down the left side of the screen. At the top of the Navigation Box there is a window for entering your search term. Type in the search term and the Navigation Box will display all occurences of the term.

There are four ways to display findings. The far left icon is for displaying a list of "Headings" created in the "Styles" section of the "Home" area. All headings other than "Normal" wll be listed here in the order of their occurance.

If you place the mouse pointer on any of the headers listed and click on it, the page will be displayed in the MS Word window for editing.

Clicking on the second icon to the right will drop mini-views of the pages with page numbers down the navigation area.

If you click on one of the mini-views, the page in the Navigation area will be outlined in yellow and be displaed in the MS Word window for editing.

Every occurance of the search word will be listed in the Navigation page in the order it occurs. The phrase containing the word is in the box and by placing the mouse pointer on the box, it displays the page number where the phrase is found.

If you click on the box where the phrase is found, the MS Word window will display the word and phrase for editing.

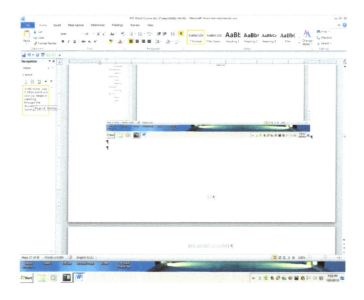

Clicking on the third icon to the right every occurance of the search word will be listed in the Navigation page in the order it occurs. The phrase containing the word is in the box and by placing the mouse pointer on the box, it displays the page number where the phrase is found.

If you click on the box where the phrase is found, the MS Word window will display the word and phrase for editing.

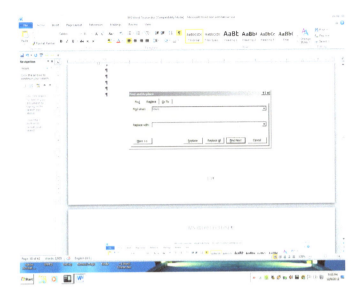

If you want to replace a word throughout, just an area,or throughout the entre document, the replace function is for you.

You can replace a word or an entire phrase by typing it in the "Find What" box in the popup.

The word or phrase to be substituted is typed into the "Replace With" window below the "Find What" window.

The "Replace" button at the bottom of the popup will replace the first occurrence of the word.

The "Replace all" button at the bottom of the popup will replace the all occurrences of the word throughout the entire document.

The "Find Next" button at the bottom of the popup will highlight each occurrence of the word one by one. This will enable you to press the "replace" button to replace only the highlighted word, or not replace the highlighted word.

Pressing the "Find Next" button will move on to the next word found.

Insert

This is the section where we insert various attributes to the pages or page contents that can't be invoked from the keyboard. These are icons or listed items that are created through the click of the mouse, or by using control characters.

Most of the attributes found in the "Insert" area will direct the reader, or user, elsewhere. Let's take a look at some of these attributes.

Pages

The "Pages" section is involved in the control of the page placement and characterization. These Icons will shape the appearance of our document to a large degree.

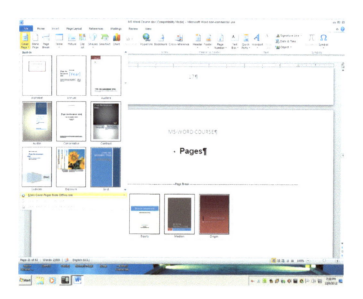

Cover Page

The "Cover Page" Icon provides the ability to create a distictful and artful cover page for your book or document. The perpose of the cover page is to provide a Title Page that makes the overall document pleasing to the eye and give the character of the document an official appearance. This can effect the credibility of the content in the mind of the observer. It takes the place of the Book Cover for documents that are not books.

Blank Page

There are times you will need a blank page, such as in publishing a bound book where the first page has to be located on the right. If the first page is determined to be on the left, the Blank Page will provide that first page move to the right by inerting the Blank Page ahead of the first page.

Page Break

This will be one of the most frequently used Icons in the MS Word banner areas. Every time you move to a new chapter or section, the previous chapter or section will be ended with a Page Break.

Clicking on the Page Break Icon will immediately end the current page and move the curser location to the top of the next page.

Tables

The "Table" area has only one Icon called "Table". If you click on the Table Icon, you can create a table in your document. More powerful than the simple ability to create a simple table is the ability to create more complex tables in your document.

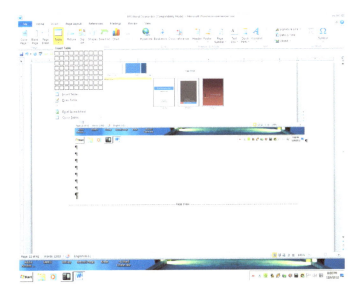

We can click on the drop-down box and insert an Excel spread sheet directly into our document and then inject the numbers and formulas needed to support our presentation.

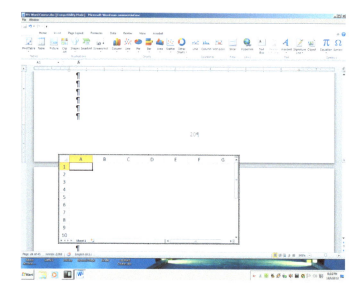

The Excel spreadsheet insertion option is shown here.

We can also click on the drop-down box and create some very powerful and complex tables. Such tables can add a whole new dimension to your books, reports and other documents.

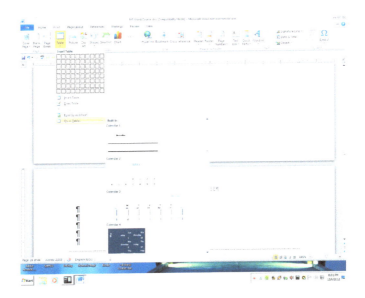

The "Quick Tables" drop-down box is shown above.

These special tables consist of Calendarsin multiple formats, Tables and Matrixes. It cuts down the effort to insert special formating to a large degree and makes your document more destictive.

Illustrations

Illustrations are an important part of many books, such as this one, where you might want to insert clipart, photos or screenshots into the text areas. Microsoft Word has an impressive array of options and add-ons for the insertion of stock and custom artwork.

Picture and Clip Art

The screenshot shown below demonstrates the Picture Icon's feature for exploring the contents of the computer to locate and insert pictures.

Use the "Insert Picture" search window to locate the picture you want to include in the document and double click on it. The picture will be inserted in the Microsoft Word document.

After you insert the photo, you can click on it and use the mouse to resize it.

If you're dealing with uploading your book to Smashwords, you should be careful to ensure that you picture is "in line with text" as shown in the screenshot below.

To do this, just place the mouse pointer on the picture and right click on the mouse. The popup shown in the photo below can be invoked by clicking on the bottom most command, "Format Picture". The resulting popup has the headers shown in the screenshot.

Click on the tab "Layout" and the options will appear. Make sure the frame is around the photo described as "in line with text" for the "Wrapping Text" mode.

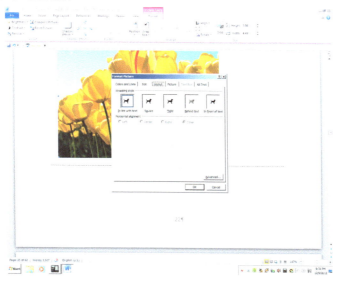

Shapes

You can create shapes right here in the Microsoft Word 2010 document with the "Shapes" dropdown box. It's somewhat reminiscent of Wing Digs with all the shapes and symbols. The shapes dropdown box is shown in the illustration below.

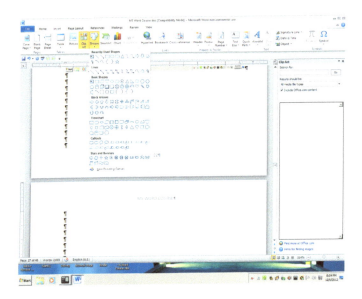

SmartArt

Just one Icon over from the shapes area is the "SmartArt" Icon. This Icon gives you the ability to create Org-Charts and more.

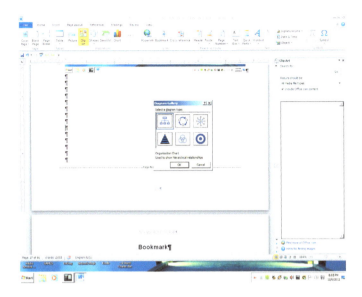

The various standard box and diagram arrays enable you to enhance your document without having to resort to complex artwork, photo capture, printing and scanning in order to get your message in the document.

Chart

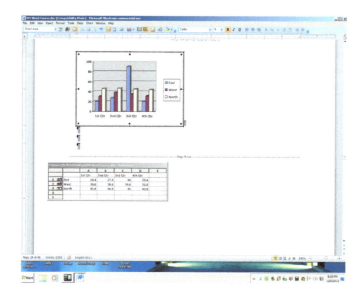

Screenshots

Screenshots are easiest inserted into your document by using the system feature rather than the Microsoft Icon for that purpose.

On your keyboard along the row of the function keys and numbers, there is a key called "Print Screen".

Press the Print Screen key and then put the curser on the place in the Microsoft Document where you want to place the screenshot.

Hold down the "Control Key" while you press the "v" key. And a picture of the screen will be inserted in the document.

Links

The Links Section is important because it enables you to connect to various areas. Both within and without the document, between bookmarks and Hyperlinks, there is nowhere you can't go.

When writing for Smashwords, the Link area is one you will use to create your table of contents through the use of the Bookmark.

Hyperlink

When creating an Internet Hyperlink, there is no need to go through the Hyperlink popup menu. The link can be made simply by using the http:// format, or the @ sign in conjunction with an Email address.

Microsoft word has had to deal with the concept of Hyperlinks within the Word document for the purposes of creating menus and redirecting the user in between and through the web pages.

The popup menu for creating menu selections within the document is the main thrust of our work here. While documents may call web sites, they rarely call other documents. When creating a menu, even a menu created using Bookmarks, the return to the Table of Contents header is generally achieved using the Hyperlink, not the Bookmark.

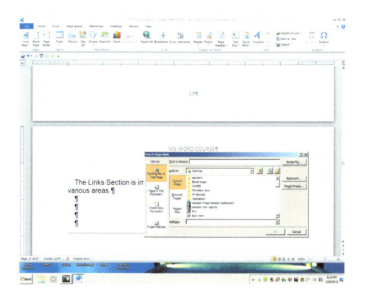

So the top "Link to" box sends the user to the "Existing File or Web Page", as shown above, the next box down, "Place in this Document" is more often used for menu items as shown in the screenshot below.

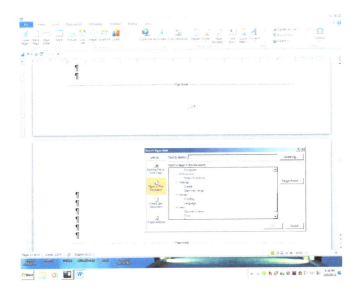

The third box down, as shown in the screenshot above, is used when creating a new document. Something you won't be doing in the content of your EBook or Paperback.

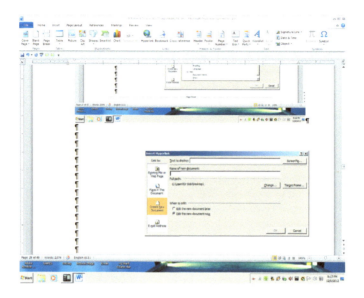

The screenshot shown below is for the creation of a link to an Email address external to the document. Such pointers are frequently used to direct the reader to a source on the Internet for obtaining products mentioned in the book or document.

The screenshot containing the popup box for the external Hyperlink is shown below.

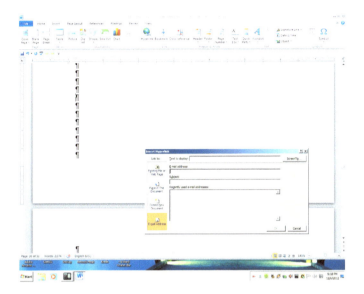

Bookmark

Bookmarks are used in some of the EBook Publisher's documents, such as Smashwords Publishing, for example.

To create a linked Table of Contents for a publisher such as Smashwords, just follow the instructions in this section.

First, create your table of contents where you want it by typing it out.

As you type out your Table of Content items, make sure your text is in the Normal paragraph style.

DO NOT create your Table of Contents in a HEADING STYLE or you will get errors when you upload your document and it will be rejected.

Avoid adding empty paragraph returns.

Only add items you intend to hyperlink.

Here's what your Table of Contents might look like:

Table of Contents

Chapter 1 – The Beginning
Chapter 2 – The Middle
Chapter 3 – More in the Middle
Chapter 4 – The Final Chapter
Etc…

Never indent your Table of Contents more than one inch from the left margin or you will get some spooky results when you try to submit your document.

ADDING BOOKMARKS:

DO NOT LINK to Word's auto-generated Heading bookmarks, create your own Bookmarks.

Go through your document, and at each Chapter Start or section heading, you will highlight the words and then select **Insert: Bookmark**.

Name your bookmark corresponding to the Chapter/Indexed item and then click add.

Bookmark names cannot have spaces or odd characters. Use only alphanumeric characters (the letters a-z or the numbers 0-9).

Repeat the process above for each and every Chapter.

TABLE OF CONTENTS

Next, return to your table of contents and highlight the phrase "Table of Contents."

Click **Insert**, **Bookmark**, and label this last bookmark something like "ref_TOC"

LINKING TO BOOKMARKS (AKA "Targeting your bookmarks)

Next, you will create your hyperlinked ToC by linking your ToC items to your target bookmarks. Highlight the text of your ToC item, such as "Chapter Five:

Right mouse click, click **Hyperlink**, then in Word's Hyperlink menu on the left hand side, click **"Place in this document."**

Select your bookmark and then click ok. Repeat this procedure for every bookmarked chapter or item in the ToC for which you want to create a clickable link.

LINKING BODY PARTS BACK UP TO THE TOP

Now you can link your chapter and section headings in your body back up to the table of contents.

Insert text as a linkable item, such as, "back to top."

Link back up to the ToC:

1. From your ToC, click on the link to jump to your chapter or section heading target.

2. After you click from your ToC to the target item's bookmark, highlight the text of item with your mouse

3. Next, click Insert: Hyperlink, and then select "Place in this document."

4. The bookmarks will appear in the main window. Select the bookmark labeled "ref_TOC,"

Header and Footer

Header

Header and footers are used to place redundant information at the top of each page. There are options around the content. The bottom of each page is customarily used for the page count.

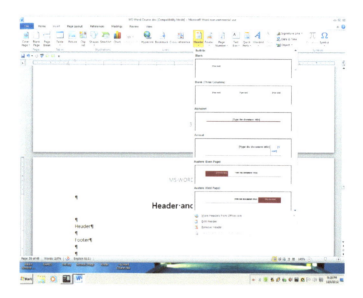

The variety of options with the content at the top of each page will cause you to need some thought around the placement of information along the top. The Header drop down box is shown above. My personal rule with regard to headers and footers is to keep it simple. Unless you have a complicated formatting situation, try to avoid excessive header and footer information.

Some books have the name of the book centered on the top of each page, while others will pit the name of the book on the upper left of the left, or even page and the author's name at the top right of the right hand, or odd page numbers.

Bear in mind that EBooks must not have anything on the top and bottom pages, because the pages are not clearly defined.

With page numbers in an EBook, depending on the font size and model of the reader, the pages will differ in length. The menu is link driven without page numbers.

Footer

The same situation exists with regard to the footers on each page. There must be no footers defined where an EBook is concerned.

When a Paperback or Hardcover book is being formatted, the page numbers traditionally go at the bottom of each page.

Footers are more complex to organize because of the need to insert section breaks in the book.

Section breaks are covered in the page layout section of this book. For now, let's quickly go over the pagination and other options and then readdress just how to properly section off and paginate your book.

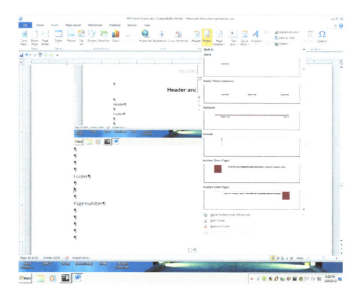

The footer drop down box is shown above. As I've already said, try to keep it simple. In fact, I try to not use the drop down box at all. I simply set the mouse pointer in the footer area of the page and then double click. Then, with my curser on the footer at the bottom of the page, I set up the page numbers without regard for the footer drop down box.

We can talk more about pagination when we get to the appropriate areas of the "Page Setup" area in the "Page Layout" section.

Page number

Once you have established the location for the page numbers, it's easy to get them posted sequentially on every page. I often just go ahead and insert the page numbers at the bottom center of every page even though I'll have to make adjustments later. It saves you from having to come back here and insert them.

One place I always stay away from is the placement of the page numbers in the "Page Margins", but such styles of formatting are a matter of personal choice. It's your book, after all.

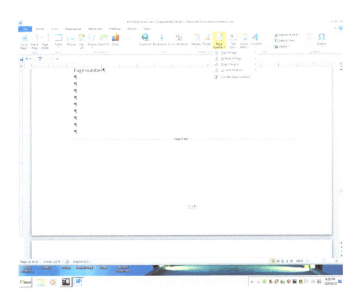

The "Format Page Numbers" item on the drop down box is something you'll always have to use if you're publishing printed books. This is a good time to get the page numbers in place.

When we get to the "Page Layout" section, we can deal with the dividing of the book into the two sections. Don't worry about the "Page Layout" for now. It will be easy to deal with when we get to that area.

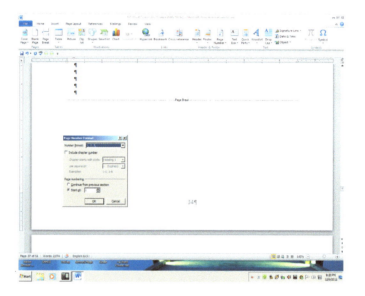

The Page numbering popup has a lot of options for numbering, but for now, let's just let the default values remain unchanged. The popup for the pagination of the book is shown above.

Page Layout

"Page Layout" issues are among some of the most important in book building. There aren't a lot of page layout issues to worry about, but the few that exist need to be addressed before the book can be published.

Let's take a look at some of the few items in the "Page Layout" area. Some of the factors affected by the page layout are the number of pages. Changing the margins and the top and bottom spacing can have a dramatic effect on the page count.

This is a good time to mention that whenever you make changes to the page count, you can be assured that the menu needs to be repaginated if you're working on a printed volume.

Page setup

Page Layout and Page Setup sound so much alike. But the "page Layout" is more concerned with the appearance of the overall document while the "Page Setup" area is devoted specifically to the placement of the text within the document.

Margins

When you click on the Margin Icon, the drop down box presents a number of options regarding the margins. The names in the drop down box offer clues as to the usage of each selection.

Whenever you see "Mirrored Margins" they apply to a document that will be in book form with left and right pages.

The insides of the facing pages are called "the gutter" by the book printing industry.

With a thicker the book the greater area of the gutter allows the book to be easier to read. That's because the book doesn't readily open up as widely as a thinner book would.

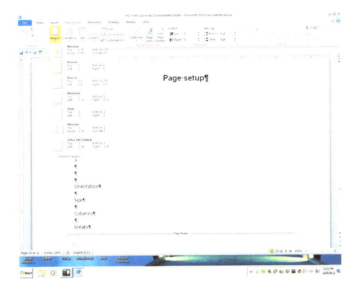

The wider the margins, the more pages a book will have.

Orientation

The "Orientation" Icon controls whether the book opens with the pages in landscape or portrait mode. Picture books or children's books will often open with the pages wader than they are tall. With pictures it allows a larger more panoramic view than with the portrait layout.

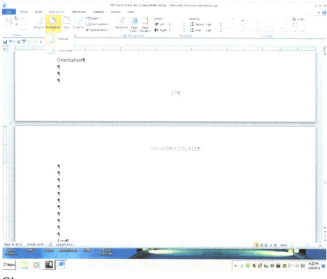

Size

I have never bothered to adjust the page size when working on a book because the standard 6″ by 9″ book size used on Internet upload areas will usually convert the 8 ½″ by 11″ pages into 6″ by 9″ automatically.

If you are converting page sizes on a book that will appear in print, once again, let me remind you that the Table of Contents will have to be repaginated. That's something the upload conversion software does not automatically do. The drop down box for page size is shown in the screenshot below.

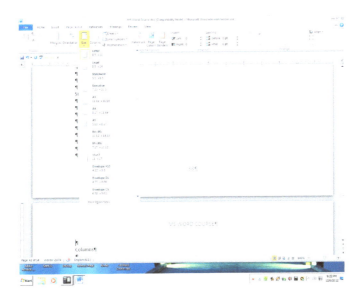

Columns

I would be tempted to say you will never have to worry about columns, but there are some exceptions that have caused me to use this feature.

If you're doing brochures and want to fold the paper in two or three columns, this can be a useful feature.

Also, if you're writing a test book, sometimes multiple columns can give a more professional appearance to the pages.

Another multi column application is the Newsletter that often comes as a stapled document and can have a more finished look when it has a multi-column structure.

The fundamental drop down box shown below has most of the basic multicolumn options listed.

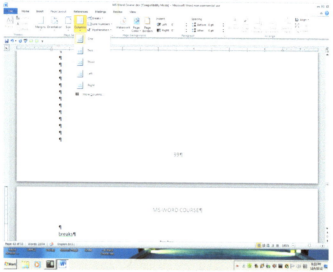

For those who need more options than are provided for in the basic drop down box, there is the option shown at the bottom of the drop down box called "More Columns", not only giving you more columns, but offering you the opportunity to select the number of columns and the spacing you desire.

This popup box shown in the screenshot below is especially useful when making brochures because it allows you the luxury of expanding the space between the columns.

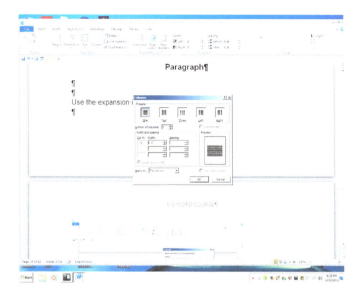

Breaks

The difference between "Page Breaks" and "Section Breaks" will become obvious when you start to work on your page numbering.

"Page Breaks" end a page and start a new page on the first line. These are used to ensure that the following page begins at the top of the page no matter when the previous page ended.

"Section Breaks" end a page and start a new page on the first line, but the Section Break also starts a new "Section" which means it's treated as a whole new document.

This is important if you want to have the first section numbered "I" through "iv" and the second section numbered "1" through "230" as you might in a book.

This is how books have separate numbers in the "Front End" and separate numbering in the rest of the book.

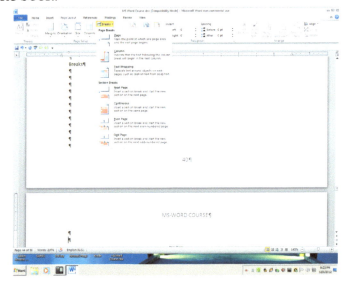

The "Page Layout".drop down box has two sections. The top section labeled "Page Breaks" is identicle to the "Page Breaks" in the "Insert" area except that the page break in the Insert Area is an immediate page break without a drop down menu. This Page Break occurs in the drop down menu with various specific funcrions.

I put this screenshot here to demonstrate that you can wrap text around a picture if you need to. Just select in "Page Setup" the Icon "Breaks" and, put the cursor after the photo on the lower right

Now click on "Text Wrapping" and next select the photo.

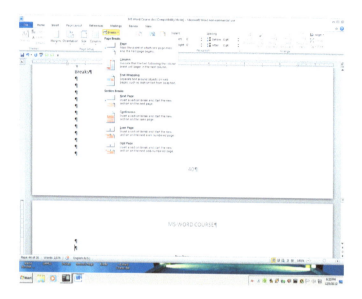

Right click on the photo and you get the popup box (not shown here) and then on the bottom section is the "Format Picture" line. When you click on the format picture line, you get the popup box shown below in the screenshot.

This is the "Format Picture" popup Box. Click on the "Layout Tab" and then select the way you want your text to wrap around the picture.

I selected "Square" and "Left" to put my picture on the left and the text square on the right of it as it appears above.

Paragraph

There are two ways to define a paragraph. One is with the Icons in the "Paragraph" section of the Home Tab, and the other is here in the "Paragraph" section of the "Page Layout" section.

If the popup box shown in the screenshot below looks familiar, it's because it is exactly the same as the popup from the "Home" section of this tutorial.

You can open the popup below using the "Expansion Icon" on the lower right corner of the "Page Setup" area.

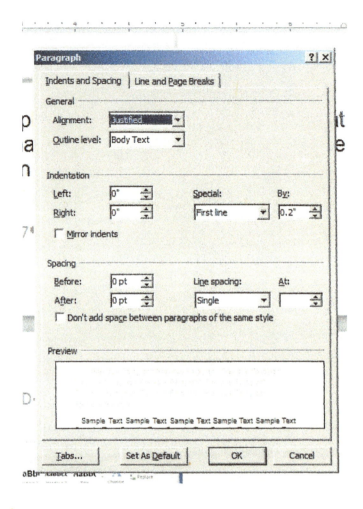

The part of the popup labeled "Indentation" is used to control the start of each paragraph. Under "Special" I select the "First Line" to set the depth of the indentation for each paragraph. You're going to want to select the best paragraph indentation for most books, which I find, at least for me, to be a "0.02" indent (The one used here in this book).

When using a paragraph indentation, there should never be a space between the paragraphs. It's not needed and makes the book look amateurish.

I do, however, use spaces between text and illustrations; otherwise I find the illustration looks crowded. Also, I use spaces to set text apart from the other items needing to be isolated.

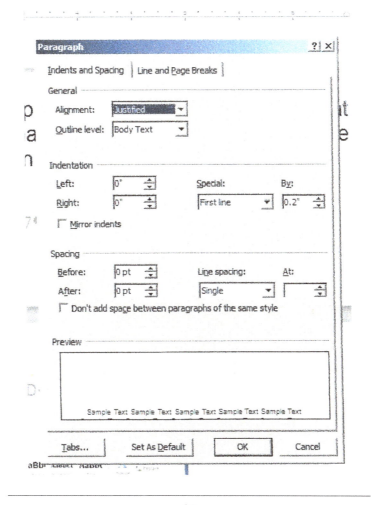

Under the section labeled, "Spacing" you will sometimes need to insert a space between paragraphs.

Textbooks are sometimes better reading with no indentation and a space between paragraphs. How-to books are also sometimes done with this format.

Never combine spacing between paragraphs with paragraph indentation. Here again, it makes the book look amateurish.

References

The "Reference" section can save you hours of work by automatically building your Table of contents. When the table of contents is constructed, it can be updated with the click of a mouse to correct page number changes caused by formatting and content changes in the document.

Table of contents

The "Table of Contents" section in the "References" area does all the magic with regard to building the type of table you need. There are two types of "Table of Contents we need to be concerned about. One is for the Paperback or Hard Cover version of your book, and the other is the EBook version of your manuscript.

Paperback and Hard Cover Table of Contents

For the Paperback or Hard Cover version of your book, click on the "Table of Contents" Icon at the far left of the "Reference" Area. The result will be a drop down menu such as the one shown below.

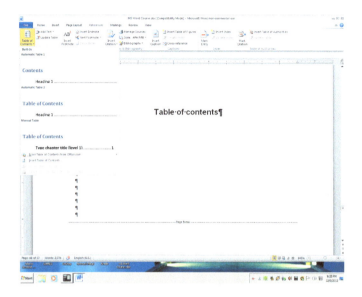

At the bottom of the drop down list, find the command labeled, "Insert Table of Contents". Clicking on this command will yield the popup box shown in the screenshot shown below.

Starting with the "Show Levels" selection in the lower left quadrant of the popup box, you will select the number of levels for your table. Level 1 is generally used for the main Paragraph Headings. A level two table, such as the one used in this book, will also allow for Sub-Paragraph Headers.

In this book, sub paragraph headers are used to take you directly to the page containing the information you're seeking. I did this because it isn't always intuitively obvious to the reader where to find the item they seek.

Other Sub-Sub-Headings are used here in a "Normal" format to break down the information further, but they aren't created using the "Level 3" setting. That's because it's always important to try and keep the menu as simple as possible.

The only thing worse than not having enough information is having so much information it becomes difficult to find your answer.

Paper Back and Hard Cover Table of Contents

Click on Table of Contents and the drop down menu appears. Go to the line item called "Insert Table of Contents and double click. This brings up the popup window shown below. There are 4 items to consider when defining you Table of Contents. They are;

1. Number of levels to be displayed in the Table of Contents, which we have described at length.

2. Whether or not you want the Page Number of the item in the Table of Contents displayed. If you are writing an EBook, you don't want page numbers.

3. Links enabled to connect the Table of Contents with a "Control" click to the item displayed.

4.   The "Tab Leader" which is the string of characters between the title name and the title Page number.

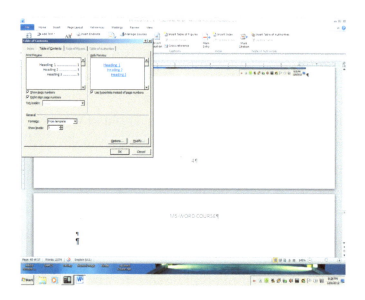

If you have already identified the Table of Contents for a Paperback or Hard Cover Book, then you need only click on the Icon called "Update Table" next to the "Table of Contents" Icon used to create the Table of Contents to be modified.

Using the update Icon can save you trouble reconfiguring the Table after making a whole new one. Bear in mind that if the Table of Contents has changed since created in any way other than the page numbers, you will have to re-create the entire Table of Contents over again.

Just one thing before we go on to the EBook menu creation. I always leave the "Link" checkbox checked even though I'm doing a numbered Table of Contents for a book. This enables me to navigate more freely around the document when using MS Word to write it.

The "Update Page Numbers" popup is shown in the screenshot below.

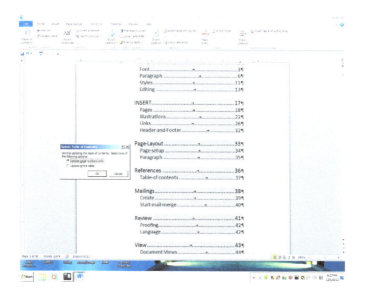

EBook Table of Contents

The two differences between the Paperback and EBook Tables of Contents in that;

The EBook must not have page numbers and the EBook must have Links to the Chapters.

And

The Paperback must have page numbers and the links to the Chapters is not required. In the final printed version the links serve no purpose.

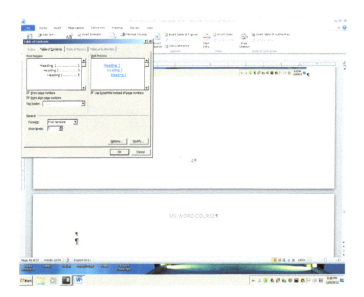

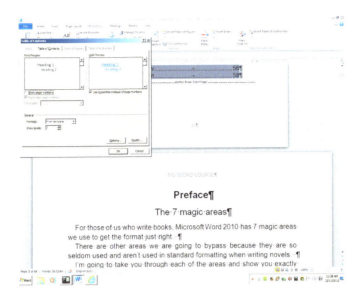

Notice that the popup in the screenshot above does not have the "Show Page Numbers" check boxes checked, while the hyperlink bix is checked.

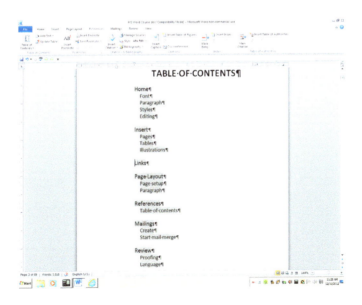

The above screenshot shows the resulting menu when creating a Table of Contents for an EBook.

Mailings

The Mailing section is probably useful if you're searching for an Agent. It can take an Agent mailing list and knock it out in a few minutes. The only disadvantage to doing a mass-mailing is the cost of postage today.

I'm finding my GoDaddy website Email service is just the ticket for mass-Emailing because of the "Template" option. You still have to send one at a time, but the body of the Email does not need to be redone.

Create

The Create area of the Mailing Section of Microsoft Word lends itself to the postal business in particular and the Labeling Icon lends itself to both the Mail and the Labeling Applications Business in general.

Envelopes

While Envelopes aren't used when publishing Paperbacks or EBooks, it's such a basic part of MS Words that I felt compelled to include it in my book.

There isn't a lot to know about printing envelopes. Just click on the "Mailings" tab and then click on the "Envelopes" Icon.

Just fill in the delivery address, or highlight the delivery address on the document page prior to going to the "Envelope" popup.

You can either leave your address in the return address field, or check the box to "Omit" your return address. Another option is to replace your return address in the return address field. If you put a new address in the return address field, you will be prompted to select it as the new return address field if so desired. You can opt to change your return address or use the new address entered and retain your original return address.

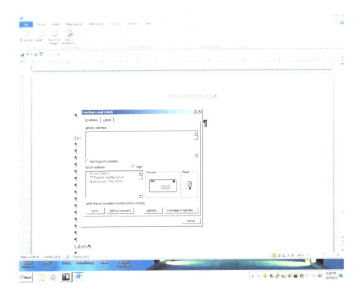

Labels

While Labels aren't used when publishing Paperbacks or EBooks, it's such a basic part of MS Words that I felt compelled to include it in my book.

Creating this document is quick and easy. If you have 500 names to enter, it's probably a pain in the neck to do by hand, but no harder than doing the mailing is without Mail Merge. The difference is you only have to do this once. The entire mailing list is shown in the screen shot above.

Here is exactly how you have to set it up. In the zoom shot below notice the top row (#1) are header names for the columns. Mail Merge will assume these are there, so if you don't put these headers in this exact place, you will lose the first row of your mailing.

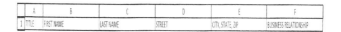

This (above) is the Excel spreadsheet with my headers in the first row across the top of the form. You need not worry about the width of the sheet because we never actually print out the actual spreadsheet; we just select fields and copy the content when merging with the mailing document.

As for the content, notice we start with the title. This column will have the titles such as, Mr., Miss, Mrs., Dr, etc. Nothing is less personal than calling a woman Mister. The observance of their title is important to personalizing your mail.

You're going to see some strange characters surrounding the mailing list words from the Excel document in this CHAPTER that you want to insert in the letter. Characters like "<<" and ">>". Don't worry about those for now. We're using these characters to point out the words we're inserting in the document.

Next, notice we have separated the first and last names into two separate columns. That's because we want the option of using the first and last names separately and multiple times in multiple ways.

Once you have a data base made you can include as many columns as you want, including financial and marketing information that can be used in a mailing, but (and here is the beautiful part) you don't have to use all of the columns. You can pick from the columns you want to include in this set of form letters and then use the same list tomorrow to mail out an entirely different letter with different columns.

So your sales solicitation letters and your thank you letters can all use the same list.

So let's fill out the mailing list using 3 names and 6 columns. You can keep adding to the list indefinitely, there is no limit.

	A	B	C	D	E	F
1	TITLE	FIRST NAME	LAST NAME	STREET	CITY, STATE, ZIP	BUSINESS RELATIONSHIP
2	Mrs.	Betty	Miller	11 Miller Lane	Benson, Al 62736	former
3	Mr.	William	Harding	22 Harding Street	Alton, SC 36283	prospective
4	Dr.	Edward	Nerdley	33 Nerdley Circle	Waycross, GA 73469	well established

This is the mailing list we will be using. There is nothing more of any real importance to know right now about using Xcel as a mailing list.

There are several more formats in many more types of lists including raw .txt formats, but why muddy the water right now? Let's just get the thing working. If you want to, you can go and pour over all the tutorials that give you the myriad of ways you can deviate from this simple approach. At least as you try other data formats, you will know the letter format is right.

FORMATTING MY LETTER

I know what you're thinking by now. If it's that easy, why do I need a "How To" tutorial? Well, everything you know how to do seems easy. The mark of a good tutorial is teaching you so well that you wonder afterwards why you needed it in the first place. So now let's start wondering why you needed to learn how to format your letter. It's going to be that easy.

Start by writing a letter as you always have, such as the one below. Please note that the red Xs below should not be included in your document. I only placed them there so you could see where the data is to be placed.

Robert Stetson
11 Eleven Eleventh Street
Circle City, ZV 99910

11/11/2011

XXXXXXXXX
XXXXXXXXX
XXXXX, XX XXXXX

Dear: XXXXX,

We thought because you are a XXXXXX customer, you might be interested in the following literature.

Shrewsbury, MA, October 10th 2012 – Robert Stetson, Has recently released a book entitled, "Abduction Avoidance and Internet Safety on Amazon's Kindle publishing.

This book is written for parents of children from infancy up to the age of 18. The advice will assist you in correcting behavioral problems in difficult to manage children and also guide the rest of us parents in protecting our young people from those who would victimize them.

It tells of how to work the system and get your child the help they need. It covers topics such as Social Services and how to use the system to your advantage. It covers "Outward Bound programs" for children with substance abuse problems and "Key Tracking" for children who disappear overnight.

You receive information on how to use the CHINS (CHild In Need of Services) system to assign people to aid you in your efforts to regain control when the child is defiant.

The book is on sale on the Amazon.com Kindle Book Store at;

http://www.amazon.com/dp/B009KXPBR0

Robert Stetson is a retired Private Detective having been licensed in both Massachusetts and Rhode Island and specializing in abductions and Internet safety. Visit his website at;

http://RobStetson.com or Email him at http://RobStetson@RobStetson.com

The actual placement of the inserted text is done by Microsoft Word. I will show you how to do it manually. The wizard that does it for you is something you can play with later in case you don't want to do it manually. If you lack the confidence to try, or just want to take the shortcut, the wizard will not spare you the work.

Leaving room for the mailing list to inject the fields you want is just the beginning. Unfortunately, Microsoft Word doesn't have a mind of its own, well sometimes it seems to doesn't it?

We have to connect the source of the data we want to insert in the letter and the letter itself.

We identify the source data file by clicking on the "Mailings" tab at the top of the Microsoft Word windows.

Click on the box labeled "Start Mail Merge" and since this is a letter, click on "letters".

Now click on the box marked "Select Recipients" and then "Use Existing List".

A window opens up with the directories such as Documents, Desktop, Disk Drives and directories. Locate your file.

When you click on your file, you will see some strange content. Ignore that. It's really your file. You can click on "Edit Recipient List" to verify the content.

Now you're ready to place the data fields in your document.

GETTING THE DATA PLACED

Click on the "Mailings" Tab at the top of the window and then click on "Start Mail Merge". Click on the "Highlight Merge Fields" icon.

Now you click on the name as it is to appear in the address field at the head of the letter. Click on the block and accept the full name. Next two lines of the address field are not shown in the window, so click in the block called "Match Fields" In the popup window.

Now you have a list of fields and the blocks going down the right side of the box line up with the content name, You want to click on "Address 1" and then "City, State, Zip" because we entered all three in one field, otherwise they would be selected separately. No change will occur in your letter because we have simply expanded the address block as shown below.

Robert Stetson
11 Eleven Eleventh Street
Circle City, ZV 99910

11/11/2011

«AddressBlock»

Dear:

We thought because you are a customer, you might be interested in the following literature.

Shrewsbury, MA, October 10th 2012 – Robert Stetson, Has recently released a book entitled, "Abduction Avoidance and Internet Safety on Amazon's Kindle publishing.

This book is written for parents of children from infancy up to the age of 18. The advice will assist you in correcting behavioral problems in difficult to manage children and also guide the rest of us parents in protecting our young people from those who would victimize them.

It tells of how to work the system and get your child the help they need. It covers topics such as Social Services and how to use the system to your advantage. It covers "Outward Bound programs" for children with substance abuse problems and "Key Tracking" for children who disappear overnight.

THE PUBLISHER'S MICROSOFT WORD

You receive information on how to use the CHINS (CHild In Need of Services) system to assign people to aid you in your efforts to regain control when the child is defiant.

The book is on sale on the Amazon.com Kindle Book Store at;

http://www.amazon.com/dp/B009KXPBR0

Robert Stetson is a retired Private Detective having been licensed in both Massachusetts and Rhode Island and specializing in abductions and Internet safety. Visit his website at;

http://RobStetson.com

or Email him at

http://RobStetson@RobStetson.com

Next place the curser (The flashing vertical line that tells you where you would type) after the word "Dear: ". Then click on "Insert Merge Field" at the top of the Microsoft Word Window. Now we have an option of how we want to address this person, whether by the first name, or by the title and past name. I have chosen to address them by their first name. When I select that as an option and click on "OK" then the following change is made in the document. The words "<<FIRST_NAME>> appear after "Dear: ".

Robert Stetson
11 Eleven Eleventh Street
Circle City, ZV 99910

11/11/2011

«AddressBlock»

Dear: «FIRST_NAME»,

We thought because you are a customer, you might be interested in the following literature.

Shrewsbury, MA, October 10th 2012 – Robert Stetson, Has recently released a book entitled, "Abduction Avoidance and Internet Safety on Amazon's Kindle publishing.

This book is written for parents of children from infancy up to the age of 18. The advice will assist you in correcting behavioral problems in difficult to manage children and also guide the rest of us parents in protecting our young people from those who would victimize them.

It tells of how to work the system and get your child the help they need. It covers topics such as Social Services and how to use the system to your advantage. It covers "Outward Bound programs" for children with substance abuse problems and "Key Tracking" for children who disappear overnight.

You receive information on how to use the CHINS (CHild In Need of Services) system to assign people to aid you in your efforts to regain control when the child is defiant.

The book is on sale on the Amazon.com Kindle Book Store at;

http://www.amazon.com/dp/B009KXPBR0

Robert Stetson is a retired Private Detective having been licensed in both Massachusetts and Rhode Island and specializing in abductions and Internet safety. Visit his website at;

http://RobStetson.com

or Email him at

http://RobStetson@RobStetson.com

Now put the curser between the word "a" and "customer" like this;

" We thought because you are a (put the curser right here) customer".

Click on the "Insert Merge Field" block at the top of the Microsoft Word Window again. And click on "Insert the Business Relationship", and then click on insert.

Notice the words "<<BUSINESS_RELATIONSHIP>> appears right between "a" and "customer. Make sure there is a space on either side of the inserted field.

Robert Stetson
11 Eleven Eleventh Street
Circle City, ZV 99910

11/11/2011

«AddressBlock»

Dear: «FIRST_NAME»,

We thought because you are a <<BUSINESS_RELATIONSHIP>> customer, you might be interested in the following literature.

Shrewsbury, MA, October 10th 2012 – Robert Stetson, Has recently released a book entitled, "Abduction Avoidance and Internet Safety on Amazon's Kindle publishing.

This book is written for parents of children from infancy up to the age of 18. The advice will assist you in correcting behavioral problems in difficult to manage children and also guide the rest of us parents in protecting our young people from those who would victimize them.

It tells of how to work the system and get your child the help they need. It covers topics such as Social Services and how to use the system to your advantage. It covers "Outward Bound programs" for children with substance abuse problems and "Key Tracking" for children who disappear overnight.

You receive information on how to use the CHINS (CHild In Need of Services) system to assign people to aid you in your efforts to regain control when the child is defiant.

The book is on sale on the Amazon.com Kindle Book Store at;

http://www.amazon.com/dp/B009KXPBR0

Robert Stetson is a retired Private Detective having been licensed in both Massachusetts and Rhode Island and specializing in abductions and Internet safety. Visit his website at;

http://RobStetson.com

or Email him at

http://RobStetson@RobStetson.com

Don't let the double carrots or the red lettering concern you. The double carrots will appear on the screen, but in their place the data field will appear. As for the red, I made the fields red here so you can pick them out easily. They will not be red when you are doing Mail Merge. Now you are ready to review the letter and the fields you have inserted. When you get the hang of it, you'll think it's a piece of cake, easy as pie, or some other popular euphemism. It should look like the letter above.

Now you're ready to run the Mail Merge and print out the stack of uniquely imprinted letters.

THE PROCESS OF MERGING

When you're done setting up the merge fields, it's best to always click on the picture of the magnifying glass over a line of text icon shown in the icons at the top of the Microsoft Word window. This will bring up the first page of your mail merge project. Examine it for errors. You don't want to print 600 copies of the letter and find out there is an error.

The project we are doing here would look like this;

MAKE THE MAILING LIST

We're going to use Excel as a basis for our Mailing List because it's the simplest way to separate the data elements for each document to be mailed. What are data elements? They are the pieces of information to be inserted in each letter, one by one. Each row in the Excel worksheet is the information needed for each letter and envelope in the mailing.

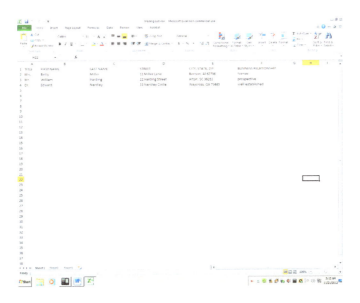

Creating this document is quick and easy. If you have 500 names to enter, it's probably a pain in the neck to do by hand, but no harder than doing the mailing is without Mail Merge. The difference is you only have to do this once. The entire mailing list is shown in the screen shot above.

Here is exactly how you have to set it up. In the zoom shot below notice the top row (#1) are header names for the columns. Mail Merge will assume these are there, so if you don't put these headers in this exact place, you will lose the first row of your mailing.

	A	B	C	D	E	F
1	TITLE	FIRST NAME	LAST NAME	STREET	CITY, STATE, ZIP	BUSINESS RELATIONSHIP

This (above) is the Excel spreadsheet with my headers in the first row across the top of the form. You need not worry about the width of the sheet because we never actually print out the actual spreadsheet; we just select fields and copy the content when merging with the mailing document.

As for the content, notice we start with the title. This column will have the titles such as, Mr., Miss, Mrs., Dr, etc. Nothing is less personal than calling a woman Mister. The observance of their title is important to personalizing your mail.

You're going to see some strange characters surrounding the mailing list words from the Excel document in this CHAPTER that you want to insert in the letter. Characters like "<<" and ">>". Don't worry about those for now. We're using these characters to point out the words we're inserting in the document.

Next, notice we have separated the first and last names into two separate columns. That's because we want the option of using the first and last names separately and multiple times in multiple ways, such as;

Dear<< John>>.

Dear << Dr.>><< Smith>>

or

<< Dr.>><< John>><< Smith>>
<< 1 Seneca Drive>>
<< San Diego, CA 90120>>

We use 8 data fields in the letter but only need 6 data fields in the mailing list.

The sixth data field I have chosen to create here is the "Relationship" data field. I'm using it to make the letter a bit more personal. It makes it less of a form letter by recognizing the person's past relationship with you. It is used like this;

We thought because you are a <<former>> customer you...

We thought because you are a <<prospective>> customer you...

We thought because you are a <<well established>> customer you…

This lead in can be personalized in order to offer special incentives or make these people feel they are part of a select group.

This flexibility can be used in other ways, such as;

Your account is now <<0>> days past due.

Your account is now <<30>> days past due.

Your account is now <<60>> days past due.

Your account is now <<90>> days past due.

This would enable you to use the mailing list for dunning purposes and reduce the hours of billing time when doing a mass mailing of bills.

Once you have a data base made you can include as many columns as you want, including financial and marketing information that can be used in a mailing, but (and here is the beautiful part) you don't have to use all of the columns. You can pick from the columns you want to include in this set of form letters and then use the same list tomorrow to mail out an entirely different letter with different columns.

So your sales solicitation letters and your thank you letters can all use the same list.

So let's fill out the mailing list using 3 names and 6 columns. You can keep adding to the list indefinitely, there is no limit.

	A	B	C	D	E	F
1	TITLE	FIRST NAME	LAST NAME	STREET	CITY, STATE, ZIP	BUSINESS RELATIONSHIP
2	Mrs.	Betty	Miller	11 Miller Lane	Benson, Al 62736	former
3	Mr.	William	Harding	22 Harding Street	Alton, SC 36283	prospective
4	Dr.	Edward	Nerdley	33 Nerdley Circle	Waycross, GA 73469	well established

This is the mailing list we will be using. There is nothing more of any real importance to know right now about using Xcel as a mailing list.

There are several more formats in many more types of lists including raw .txt formats, but why muddy the water right now? Let's just get the thing working. If you want to, you can go and pour over all the tutorials that give you the myriad of ways you can deviate from this simple approach. At least as you try other data formats, you will know the letter format is right.

FORMATTING MY LETTER

I know what you're thinking by now. If it's that easy, why do I need a "How To" tutorial? Well, everything you know how to do seems easy. The mark of a good tutorial is teaching you so well that you wonder afterwards why you needed it in the first place. So now let's start wondering why you needed to learn how to format your letter. It's going to be that easy.

Start by writing a letter as you always have, such as the one below. Please note that the red Xs below should not be included in your document. I only placed them there so you could see where the data is to be placed.

Robert Stetson
11 Eleven Eleventh Street
Circle City, ZV 99910

11/11/2011

XXXXXXXXX
XXXXXXXXX
XXXXX, XX XXXXX

Dear: XXXXX,

We thought because you are a XXXXXX customer, you might be interested in the following literature.

Shrewsbury, MA, October 10th 2012 – Robert Stetson, Has recently released a book entitled, "Abduction Avoidance and Internet Safety on Amazon's Kindle publishing.

This book is written for parents of children from infancy up to the age of 18. The advice will assist you in correcting behavioral problems in difficult to manage children and also guide the rest of us parents in protecting our young people from those who would victimize them.

It tells of how to work the system and get your child the help they need. It covers topics such as Social Services and how to use the system to your advantage. It covers "Outward Bound programs" for children with substance abuse problems and "Key Tracking" for children who disappear overnight.

You receive information on how to use the CHINS (CHild In Need of Services) system to assign people to aid you in your efforts to regain control when the child is defiant.

The book is on sale on the Amazon.com Kindle Book Store at;

http://www.amazon.com/dp/B009KXPBR0

Robert Stetson is a retired Private Detective having been licensed in both Massachusetts and Rhode Island and specializing in abductions and Internet safety. Visit his website at;

http://RobStetson.com

or Email him at

http://RobStetson@RobStetson.com

The actual placement of the inserted text is done by Microsoft Word. I will show you how to do it manually. The wizard that does it for you is something you can play with later in case you don't want to do it manually. If you lack the confidence to try, or just want to take the shortcut, the wizard will not spare you the work.

Leaving room for the mailing list to inject the fields you want is just the beginning. Unfortunately, Microsoft Word doesn't have a mind of its own, well sometimes it seems to doesn't it?

We have to connect the source of the data we want to insert in the letter and the letter itself.

We identify the source data file by clicking on the "Mailings" tab at the top of the Microsoft Word windows.

Click on the box labeled "Start Mail Merge" and since this is a letter, click on "letters".

Now click on the box marked "Select Recipients" and then "Use Existing List".

A window opens up with the directories such as Documents, Desktop, Disk Drives and directories. Locate your file.

When you click on your file, you will see some strange content. Ignore that. It's really your file. You can click on "Edit Recipient List" to verify the content.

Now you're ready to place the data fields in your document.

PLACING THE DATA

Personally, I like doing it manually, here goes.

Click on the "Mailings" Tab at the top of the window and then click on "Start Mail Merge". Click on the "Highlight Merge Fields" icon.

Now you click on the name as it is to appear in the address field at the head of the letter. Click on the block and accept the full name. Next two lines of the address field are not shown in the window, so click in the block called "Match Fields" In the popup window.

Now you have a list of fields and the blocks going down the right side of the box line up with the content name, You want to click on "Address 1" and then "City, State, Zip" because we entered all three in one field, otherwise they would be selected separately. No change will occur in your letter because we have simply expanded the address block as shown below.

Next place the curser (The flashing vertical line that tells you where you would type) after the word "Dear: ". Then click on "Insert Merge Field" at the top of the Microsoft Word Window. Now we have an option of how we want to address this person, whether by the first name, or by the title and past name. I have chosen to address them by their first name. When I select that as an option and click on "OK" then the following change is made in the document. The words "<<FIRST_NAME>> appear after "Dear: ".

Robert Stetson
11 Eleven Eleventh Street
Circle City, ZV 99910

11/11/2011

«AddressBlock»

Dear: «FIRST_NAME»,

We thought because you are a customer, you might be interested in the following literature.

Shrewsbury, MA, October 10th 2012 – Robert Stetson, Has recently released a book entitled, "Abduction Avoidance and Internet Safety on Amazon's Kindle publishing.

This book is written for parents of children from infancy up to the age of 18. The advice will assist you in correcting behavioral problems in difficult to manage children and also guide the rest of us parents in protecting our young people from those who would victimize them.

It tells of how to work the system and get your child the help they need. It covers topics such as Social Services and how to use the system to your advantage. It covers "Outward Bound programs" for children with substance abuse problems and "Key Tracking" for children who disappear overnight.

You receive information on how to use the CHINS (CHild In Need of Services) system to assign people to aid you in your efforts to regain control when the child is defiant.

The book is on sale on the Amazon.com Kindle Book Store at;

http://www.amazon.com/dp/B009KXPBR0

Robert Stetson is a retired Private Detective having been licensed in both Massachusetts and Rhode Island and specializing in abductions and Internet safety. Visit his website at;

http://RobStetson.com

or Email him at

http://RobStetson@RobStetson.com

Now put the curser between the word "a" and "customer" like this;

" We thought because you are a (put the curser right here) customer".

Click on the "Insert Merge Field" block at the top of the Microsoft Word Window again. And click on "Insert the Business Relationship", and then click on insert.

Notice the words "<<BUSINESS_RELATIONSHIP>> appears right between "a" and "customer. Make sure there is a space on either side of the inserted field.

Robert Stetson
11 Eleven Eleventh Street
Circle City, ZV 99910

11/11/2011

«AddressBlock»

Dear: «FIRST_NAME»,

We thought because you are a «BUSINESS_RELATIONSHIP» customer, you might be interested in the following literature.

Shrewsbury, MA, October 10th 2012 – Robert Stetson, Has recently released a book entitled, "Abduction Avoidance and Internet Safety on Amazon's Kindle publishing.

This book is written for parents of children from infancy up to the age of 18. The advice will assist you in correcting behavioral problems in difficult to manage children and also guide the rest of us parents in protecting our young people from those who would victimize them.

It tells of how to work the system and get your child the help they need. It covers topics such as Social Services and how to use the system to your advantage. It covers "Outward Bound programs" for children with substance abuse problems and "Key Tracking" for children who disappear overnight.

You receive information on how to use the CHINS (CHild In Need of Services) system to assign people to aid you in your efforts to regain control when the child is defiant.

The book is on sale on the Amazon.com Kindle Book Store at;

http://www.amazon.com/dp/B009KXPBR0

Robert Stetson is a retired Private Detective having been licensed in both Massachusetts and Rhode Island and specializing in abductions and Internet safety. Visit his website at;

http://RobStetson.com

or   Email   him   at

http://RobStetson@RobStetson.com

Don't let the double carrots or the red lettering concern you. The double carrots will appear on the screen, but in their place the data field will appear. As for the red, I made the fields red here so you can pick them out easily. They will not be red when you are doing Mail Merge. Now you are ready to review the letter and the fields you have inserted. When you get the hang of it, you'll think it's a piece of cake, easy as pie, or some other popular euphemism. It should look like the letter above.

Now you're ready to run the Mail Merge and print out the stack of uniquely imprinted letters.

THE PROCESS OF MERGING

When you're done setting up the merge fields, it's best to always click on the picture of the magnifying glass over a line of text icon shown in the icons at the top of the Microsoft Word window. This will bring up the first page of your mail merge project. Examine it for errors. You don't want to print 600 copies of the letter and find out there is an error.

The project we are doing here would look like this;

Robert Stetson
11 Eleven Eleventh Street
Circle City, ZV 99910

11/11/2011

Mrs. Betty Miller
11 Miller Lane
Benson, Al 62736

Dear: Betty,

We thought because you are a former customer, you might be interested in the following literature.

Shrewsbury, MA, October 10th 2012 – Robert Stetson, Has recently released a book entitled, "Abduction Avoidance and Internet Safety on Amazon's Kindle publishing.

This book is written for parents of children from infancy up to the age of 18. The advice will assist you in correcting behavioral problems in difficult to manage children and also guide the rest of us parents in protecting our young people from those who would victimize them.

It tells of how to work the system and get your child the help they need. It covers topics such as Social Services and how to use the system to your advantage. It covers "Outward Bound programs" for children with substance abuse problems and "Key Tracking" for children who disappear overnight.

You receive information on how to use the CHINS (CHild In Need of Services) system to assign people to aid you in your efforts to regain control when the child is defiant.

The book is on sale on the Amazon.com Kindle Book Store at;

http://www.amazon.com/dp/B009KXPBR0

Robert Stetson is a retired Private Detective having been licensed in both Massachusetts and Rhode Island and specializing in abductions and Internet safety. Visit his website at;

http://RobStetson.com

or   Email   him   at
http://RobStetson@RobStetson.com

PRINT THE MAILINGS

THIS IS VERY IMPORTANT: Make sure that you save the letter document under the current document name and then under a different name. This will prevent the loss of the original document when the labels are printed.

Click on the "Mailings" tab if you're not already in the Mailings Menu. Click on the "Finish & Merge" field at the top of the Microsoft Window and then a menu will drop down. Now click on "Print Documents" and the print process will be enabled.

A popup box appears and gives you 3 options. These are;

All

Current Record

From ___ to ___

"All" will print the entire mailing List, Merging the entire data list with the letter.

"Current Record" will print only the record you are looking at on the screen.

"From ___ to ___ will print any range of records from the record number you select (From) to the record you chose as the stopping point (To).

Now: how to change individual copies of the document

On the Mailings tab, in the Finish & Merge group, click on Finish & Merge, and then click on Edit Individual Documents.

Choose whether you want to edit the whole set of documents, only the copy that's currently visible, or a subset of the set, which you specify by record number. Word compiles the copies that you want to edit into a single file, with a page break between each copy of the document.

After you finish editing the new file of documents, you can print the documents by clicking the File tab, clicking on Print, and then clicking on the Print button.

Save the main document

Remember that merged documents that you save are separate from the main document. It's a good idea to save the main document itself if you plan to use it for another mail merge. That's because once you finish the merge, the original document is gone.

When you save the main document, you also save its connection to the data file. The next time that you open the main document, you are prompted to choose whether you want the information from the data file to be merged again into the main document.

If you click on, "Yes", the document opens with information from the first record merged in.

If you click on, "No", the connection between the main document and the data file is broken. The main document becomes a standard Word document. Fields are replaced with the unique information from the first record.

Robert Stetson
11 Eleven Eleventh Street
Circle City, ZV 99910

11/11/2011

Mrs. Betty Miller
11 Miller Lane
Benson, Al 62736

Dear: Betty,

We thought because you are a former customer, you might be interested in the following literature.

Shrewsbury, MA, October 10th 2012 – Robert Stetson, Has recently released a book entitled, "Abduction Avoidance and Internet Safety on Amazon's Kindle publishing.

This book is written for parents of children from infancy up to the age of 18. The advice will assist you in correcting behavioral problems in difficult to manage children and also guide the rest of us parents in protecting our young people from those who would victimize them.

It tells of how to work the system and get your child the help they need. It covers topics such as Social Services and how to use the system to your advantage. It covers "Outward Bound programs" for children with substance abuse problems and "Key Tracking" for children who disappear overnight.

You receive information on how to use the CHINS (CHild In Need of Services) system to assign people to aid you in your efforts to regain control when the child is defiant.

The book is on sale on the Amazon.com Kindle Book Store at;

http://www.amazon.com/dp/B009KXPBR0

Robert Stetson is a retired Private Detective having been licensed in both Massachusetts and Rhode Island and specializing in abductions and Internet safety. Visit his website at;

http://RobStetson.com

or   Email   him   at
http://RobStetson@RobStetson.com

THE PUBLISHER'S MICROSOFT WORD

PRINT THE MAILINGS

THIS IS VERY IMPORTANT: Make sure that you save the letter document under the current document name and then under a different name. This will prevent the loss of the original document when the labels are printed.

Click on the "Mailings" tab if you're not already in the Mailings Menu. Click on the "Finish & Merge" field at the top of the Microsoft Window and then a menu will drop down. Now click on "Print Documents" and the print process will be enabled.

A popup box appears and gives you 3 options. These are;

All

Current Record

From ___ to ___

"All" will print the entire mailing List, Merging the entire data list with the letter.

"Current Record" will print only the record you are looking at on the screen.

"From ___ to ___ will print any range of records from the record number you select (From) to the record you chose as the stopping point (To).

Now: how to change individual copies of the document

On the Mailings tab, in the Finish & Merge group, click on Finish & Merge, and then click on Edit Individual Documents.

Choose whether you want to edit the whole set of documents, only the copy that's currently visible, or a subset of the set, which you specify by record number. Word compiles the copies that you want to edit into a single file, with a page break between each copy of the document.

After you finish editing the new file of documents, you can print the documents by clicking the File tab, clicking on Print, and then clicking on the Print button.

Save the main document

Remember that merged documents that you save are separate from the main document. It's a good idea to save the main document itself if you plan to use it for another mail merge. That's because once you finish the merge, the original document is gone.

When you save the main document, you also save its connection to the data file. The next time that you open the main document, you are prompted to choose whether you want the information from the data file to be merged again into the main document.

If you click on, "Yes", the document opens with information from the first record merged in.

If you click on, "No", the connection between the main document and the data file is broken. The main document becomes a standard Word document. Fields are replaced with the unique information from the first record.

Review Area

The "Review" area isn't used by everyone. The use of comments is somewhat ambiguous in light of the fact that you are creating a book or document for publication. Inclusion of comments in a works for submission will inhibit the translator's ability to convert he book to the many platforms it's to be published on.

The comments feature is mostly useful when reviewing someone else's work that has been submitted to be reviewed by you.

Proofing

Proofing is useful if the automated features are not active in your Word document, where your document is the subject of review. You won't normally use the Proofing section to review your own documents, but rather the documents submitted to you by others. One exception is the thesaurus that opens up the column on the right side of the screen for researching the word you wish to examine.

Clicking on the "Thesaurus" Icon will also turn on the "Research" Icon and has much the same function.

Spell check

The Spell Checker is rather redundant because of the integrated spell checker in the word processor. One exception is to check the spelling in a document you have received for review from another person.

It will check both the spelling and the grammar in documents you did not create. The "Word Counter" is also useful when evaluating work that has been submitted by another person for your review.

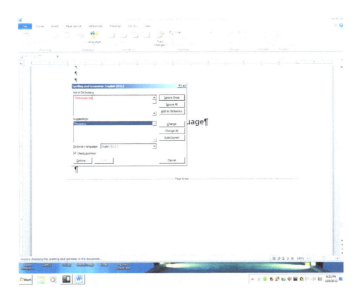

Above is a screenshot of the "Spelling & Grammar" popup which is invoked by the "Spelling & Grammar" Icon in the "Proofing" section.

Research

The "Research" Icon can be a useful tool, but I've usually completed my research before beginning my book.

Thesaurus

The Thesaurus can be a useful tool when you need to find that special word to describe a particular scenario or to avoid redundancy by the use of a recurring adjective.

Use the Thesaurus freely as an aid. The screenshot for the Research and Thesaurus Icons is shown below.

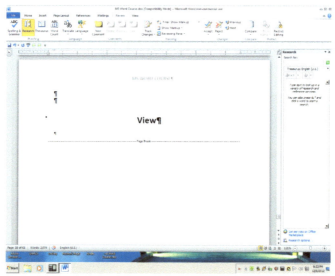

The screenshot above shows the right hand column which is used for both the Research and the Thesaurus Icons. The right hand column does double duty in these two functions.

Word count

The MS Word document also has a word counter, page counter and an Icon on the bottom of the page to let you know if there are any issues in your document when you are creating a document of your own.

This Word Count feature is primarily for getting a word count on documents submitted for review by you. The entire "Review" area is intended for doing reviews, not original document creation.

There is an option to include or omit textboxes, footnotes and endnotes by clicking on the checkbox at the bottom of the popup.

The "Word Count" popup is shown in the screenshot below. It's function includes not only word count, but character count both with and without spaces, paragraph count and page count along with the number of lines in the document.

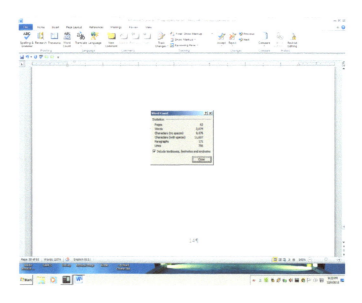

Language

The "Language" section has a translator and a language selection Icon to identify the source and destination languages for the translator. The Language section has an Icon called "Language" that can make it somewhat confusing to the reader. With reference to the "Language" Icon, clicking on it will cause a drop down menu to appear.

The drop down menu is shown in the screenshot below and gives you three options to choose from. These options are described below the screenshot.

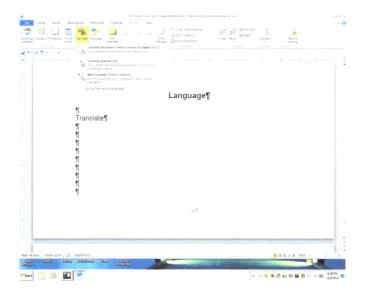

Translate Document

This option allows the user to translate a document from one language to another.

Translate Selected Text

If there is a section or a word that is new to you, you can use the "Translate Selected Text" option as a multilingual dictionary to decipher the meaning of a word.

Mini-Translator

This little popup gem is a bit of a pain in the neck. As you invoke it as an option, it gives little popups when your mouse pointer touches a word and gives you the translation. If you're working in your native language and you have the translator set to translate to another language, the popup will haunt you with popups containing the equivalent word in the other language while you're trying to write. Don't forget to turn it off if you're done with it.

Choose Transition Language

This is the setting for selecting, after you define your native language", the "other" language.

Language

Microsoft maintains online language translation banks for your convenience. I'm impressed with the scope and depth of this database. It's worth a fortune and would have been prohibitively expensive years ago.

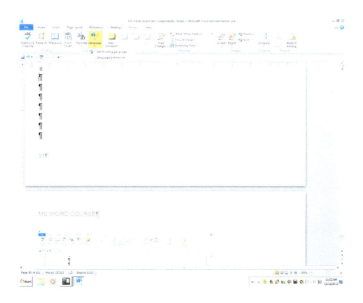

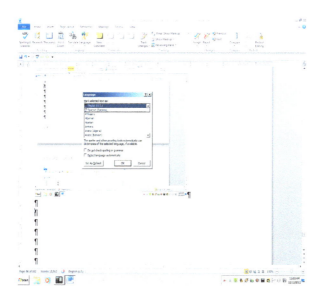

If you click on the "Language" Icon you will see the vast array of languages offered by Microsoft as an extension of their word processor. The popup listing these languages is shown in the screenshot below.

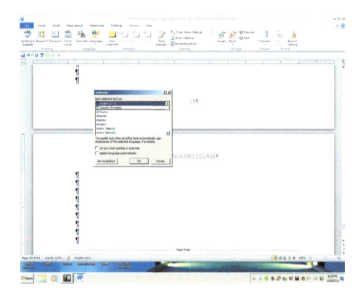

You can set your Microsoft Office Preferences using the popup box below. If you require transition languages you should obtain a Microsoft Word Users Guide from Microsoft. The scope and depth of the topic is too broad and too deep for this guide, which focuses on the use of Microsoft Word for the Book Writer, not for the translator.

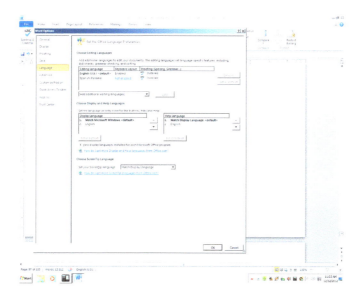

View

The View area is mainly concerned with the appearance of the document on the screen or with the printing of the document. We're going to spend some time on each point because they add a bit of comfort to your writing.

Show

The "Show" section is one of the more useful areas in the MS Word lineup. It contains the "Ruler" checkbox that allows you to either display the ruler at the top and side of the word document.

Ruler

The ruler enables multiple benefits, but is usually ignored by writers. The full value of the ruler is realized when inserting photos, charts or screenshots into your document.

I actually wish they had put this feature in either the "Insert" or the "Page Layout" area so it would be more easily found.

There is a screenshot displayed below of the Microsoft Word screen with the ruler showing on the top and side of the page. If you have a ruler displayed, you will have both the vertical and horizontal rulers on the screen.

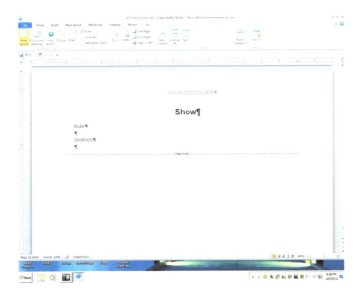

Gridlines

The gridlines have a purpose. They can work with the picture sizing task or they can work with the "Shapes" feature. Also they can work with inserted Calendars, pictures and graphs.

I have turned on the gridlines in the screenshot below.

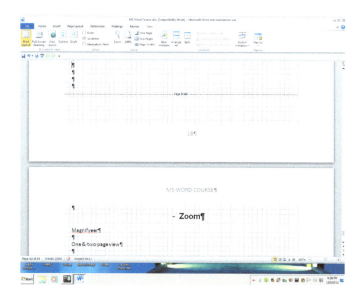

Navigation Pane

The "Navigation Pane" allows you to transport your curser and page view to any part of the document with ease.

Listed in the Navigation Pane are the various heading levels. The lower levels being indented proportionately. Think of it as an active EBook menu where you select your location by selecting the menu item on the page.

When you're creating a document with several "Header Levels", the Navigation Pane will show you the level of the item you're working on, so if you make an error on a document header, you can correct the mistake.

I have provided a screenshot below of the Navigation Pane showing the pane down the left hand side of the document with Header Level content.

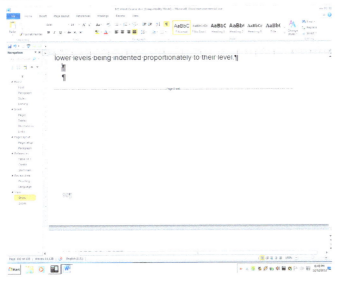

Zoom

Here again the Area and the Section name are the same. The "Zoom Area" encompasses the document views, Show, Zoom, Window and Macros, while the "Zoom Section" limits its scope to the size of the window used by Microsoft Word.

Zoom

The Zoom Section is invoked by clicking on the magnifying glass picture. It puts up a popup for sizing the window. The screenshot is shown below. I like to opt for the maximum page width because it's easier on the eyes.

The maximum page width can be found by clicking on the "Page Width" bullet at the top middle of the screen. The "Percent" window allows you to declare the percentage of the screen window you want. I use 150%, which might seem odd, except it allows 100% of the screen to display a single page width.

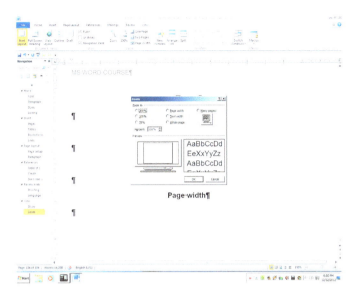

One & two page view

The two page view is shown below and can make the reading of a book more true to life. Also in books or documents where illustrations span two pages, it can allow you to see both halves of the picture.

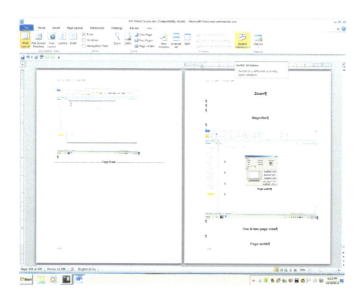

Page width

The "Page Width" Icon allows you to toggle the page width from wide to narrow and back. This is useful when comparing two documents using two different Microsoft Word documents, or when comparing the content of a Word document on the same screen as an Adobe document.

Using the Page Width option can allow you to see the entire width of the word document even though it's only as wide as half the screen.

ABOUT THE AUTHOR

I am a retired hardware and software Engineer with a background in Law Enforcement and real estate brokerage.

Log onto my Web Site for a link to Amazon.Com special deals and for information on other books I have written;

http://WWW.RobStetson.Com

www.ingramcontent.com/pod-product-compliance
Lightning Source LLC
LaVergne TN
LVHW012315070326
832902LV00001BA/4